William Pharazyn

A Collection of Acts of the Imperial Parliament

Affecting the Constitution of New Zealand

William Pharazyn

A Collection of Acts of the Imperial Parliament
Affecting the Constitution of New Zealand

ISBN/EAN: 9783337151324

Printed in Europe, USA, Canada, Australia, Japan

Cover: Foto ©Suzi / pixelio.de

More available books at **www.hansebooks.com**

A COLLECTION

OF

ACTS OF THE IMPERIAL PARLIAMENT

AFFECTING

THE CONSTITUTION OF NEW ZEALAND.

PREPARED FOR PUBLICATION UNDER THE DIRECTION OF THE GOVERNMENT

BY

WILLIAM PHARAZYN,

Assistant Law Officer.

NEW ZEALAND:

BY AUTHORITY: GEORGE DIDSBURY, GOVERNMENT PRINTER, WELLINGTON.

1870.

ACTS OF THE IMPERIAL PARLIAMENT

AFFECTING

THE CONSTITUTION OF NEW ZEALAND.

THE CONSTITUTION ACT.(¹)

(15 & 16 VICT. c. 72.)

AN ACT *to grant a Representative Constitution to the Colony of New Zealand.* [30th June, 1852.]

WHEREAS by an Act of the Session holden in the third 3 and 4 Vict. and fourth years of Her Majesty, chapter sixty-two, it c. 62. was enacted, that it should be lawful for Her Majesty, by Letters Patent, to be from time to time issued under the Great Seal of the United Kingdom, to erect into a separate Colony or Colonies any Islands which then were, or which thereafter might be, comprised within and be Dependencies of the Colony of New South Wales : And whereas in pursuance of the powers in Her vested by the said Act, Her Majesty did, by certain Letters Patent under the Great Seal of the United Kingdom, bearing date the sixteenth day of November, in the fourth year of Her reign, erect into a separate Colony the Islands of New Zealand, theretofore comprised within or Dependencies of the Colony of New South Wales, bounded as therein described ; and the said Islands of New Zealand were thereby erected into a separate Colony accordingly ; and Her Majesty did, by the said Letters Patent, authorize the Governor for the time being of the said Colony of New Zealand, and certain other persons, to be a Legislative Council for such Colony, and to make laws for the peace, order, and good government thereof : And whereas by an 9 and 10 Vict. Act of the Session holden in the ninth and tenth years c. 103.

(¹) This title is given by the Interpretation Acts 1858 and 1868. The Act was proclaimed in New Zealand on the 17th January, 1853.

of Her Majesty, chapter one hundred and three, the Act firstly herein recited, and all Charters, Letters Patent, Instructions, and Orders in Council, made and issued in pursuance thereof, were repealed, abrogated, and annulled, so far as the same were repugnant to the Act now in recital, or any Letters Patent, Charters, Orders in Council, or Royal Instructions to be issued under the authority thereof; and, by the Act now in recital, certain powers for the government of the said Islands were vested in Her Majesty, to be executed by Letters Patent under the Great Seal of the United Kingdom, or by Instructions under Her Majesty's signet and sign manual, approved in Her Privy Council, and accompanying or referred to in such Letters Patent : And whereas in pursuance of the said last-mentioned Act, Her Majesty did, by Letters Patent, bearing date at Westminster the twenty-third day of December, in the tenth year of Her reign, and by certain instructions made and approved as required by such Act, and bearing even date with and accompanying the said Letters Patent, execute certain of the powers by such Act vested in Her Majesty for the better

11 and 12 Vict. c. 5.

government of the said Islands :   And whereas by an Act of the Session holden in the eleventh and twelfth years of Her Majesty, chapter five, so much of the said Act secondly herein recited, and the said Letters Patent and Instructions issued in pursuance thereof, as relates to the constitution and establishment of two or more separate Assemblies within the said Islands, and of a General Assembly in and for the said Islands, was suspended for five years, unless Her Majesty, with the advice of Her Privy Council, should direct the same to be carried into effect before the expiration of that period ; and, by the Act now in recital, the said firstly-recited Act, Letters Patent, and Instructions were revived for the time during which the said secondly recited Act, Letters Patent, and Instructions were suspended as aforesaid ; and, by the Act now in recital, certain powers were vested respectively in the Governor-in-Chief of the said Islands, and in such Governor and the Legislative Council thereof : And whereas it is expedient that further and better provision should be made for the Government of New Zealand :

BE IT THEREFORE ENACTED by the Queen's most excellent Majesty, by and with the advice and consent of the Lords Spiritual and Temporal, and Commons in this present Parliament assembled, and by the authority of the same, as follows :—

1. The said Acts, and all Charters, Letters Patent, Instructions, and Orders in Council, issued in pursuance thereof, shall be, and the same are hereby repealed, so far as the same are repugnant to, or would prevent or interfere with the operation of this Act, or any Letters Patent or Instructions to be issued under the authority or in pursuance of this Act: Provided nevertheless, that all laws and ordinances made, and acts done, under and in pursuance of the said recited Acts, and any Charters, Letters Patent, Instructions, or Orders in Council, issued in pursuance thereof, shall continue as lawful, valid, and effectual, as if this Act had not been passed, save so far as any such laws, ordinances, or acts may be repugnant to, or would prevent or interfere with, the operation of this Act: Provided also, that, until the expiration of the time, or latest of the times, appointed for the return of writs for the first election of Members of the Provincial Councils of the Provinces established by this Act, the existing Provincial Legislative Councils shall continue to have and exercise all rights, jurisdiction, powers, and authorities which they would have had if this Act had not been passed; and until the expiration of the time appointed for the return of the writs for the first election of the Members of the House of Representatives to be constituted under this Act, the Legislative Council of New Zealand shall continue to have and exercise all rights, jurisdiction, powers, and authorities which such Legislative Council would have had if this Act had not been passed.

Repeal of recited Acts, &c.

Provisoes.

2. The following Provinces are hereby established in New Zealand, namely, Auckland, New Plymouth,(¹)

Certain Provinces established in New Zealand.

(¹) See section 69, *post*. The name of New Plymouth was changed to Taranaki by "The Province of Taranaki Act, 1858." By Proclamation of 28th February, 1853, the boundaries of the several Provinces were defined as follows :—" The Province of *Auckland* shall be bounded on the North by the coast line, including the islands adjacent thereto ; the East by the coast line, including the islands adjacent thereto ; the West by the coast line, including the islands adjacent thereto ; the South by the River Mokau to its source, thence by a right line running

Wellington, Nelson, Canterbury, and Otago; and the limits of such several Provinces shall be fixed by Proclamation by the Governor, as soon as conveniently may be after the proclamation of this Act in New Zealand.

Each Province to have a Superintendent and Provincial Council.
3. For each of the said Provinces hereby established, and for every Province hereafter to be established as hereinafter provided, there shall be a Superintendent and a Provincial Council; and the Provincial Council of each of the said Provinces hereby established shall consist of such number of Members, not less than nine, as the Governor shall by proclamation direct and appoint.

Before elections of Members of Provincial Councils, Superintendents of Provinces to be chosen.
4. Upon or before the issue of writs for the first election of Members of the Provincial Council for any Province established by or under this Act, the persons duly qualified in each of the said Provinces to elect Members of the Provincial Councils as hereinafter mentioned, shall elect a Superintendent of such Province; and on the termination of such Council, by

from the source of the Mokau to the point where the Ngahuinga or Tuhua, the principal tributary of the Whanganui River, is intersected by the thirty-ninth parallel of South latitude, thence eastward by the thirty-ninth parallel of South latitude to the point where that parallel of latitude cuts the east coast of the Northern Island of New Zealand. The Province of *New Plymouth* shall be bounded on the North by the River Mokau to its source; the East by a right line running from the source of the River Mokau to the point where the Ngahuinga or Tuhua, the principal tributary of the Whanganui River, is intersected by the thirty-ninth parallel of South latitude, thence by the River Whanganui to the point where it is met by the Taumatamahoe path leading from the River Waitera, thence by a right line running from the above-described point on the Whanganui River to the mouth of the River Patea; the West by the coast line, including the islands adjacent thereto; the South by the coast line, including the islands adjacent thereto. The Province of *Wellington* shall be bounded on the North by the southern boundary of the Province of Auckland, as already described in this Proclamation; the East by the coast line, including the islands adjacent thereto; the North-west by the southern portion of the eastern boundary of the Province of New Plymouth, as already described in this Proclamation; the South-west by the coast line, including the islands adjacent thereto; the South by the coast line, including the islands adjacent thereto. The Province of *Nelson* shall be bounded on the North by the coast line, including the islands adjacent thereto; the East by the coast line, including the islands adjacent thereto; the West by the coast line, including the islands adjacent thereto; the South by the River Hurunui to its source, thence by a right line drawn to the point where the River Kotuurakaoka issues out of Lake Brunner, thence by the River Kotu-

expiration of the period hereinafter fixed for its continuance, or by the previous dissolution thereof, the persons qualified as aforesaid shall elect the same or some other person to be Superintendent, and so on from time to time; and every such Superintendent shall hold his office until the election of his successor: Provided always,([1]) that it shall be lawful for the Governor of New Zealand, on behalf of Her Majesty, to disallow any such election; and if such disallowance be signified by the Governor, under the Seal of New Zealand, to the Speaker of such Council, at any time within three months after such election, the office of Superintendent shall become vacant;([2]) and on any vacancy occasioned by such disallowance, or by the death or resignation of the Superintendent (such resignation being accepted by the Governor on behalf of Her Majesty), a new election shall in like manner take place: Provided further, that, at any time during the continuance of the office of any such Superintendent, it shall be lawful for Her Majesty to remove him from such office, on receiving an address

---

urakaoka to its junction with the River Grey, thence by the River Grey to its mouth. The Province of *Canterbury* shall be bounded on the North by the southern boundary of the Province of Nelson, as already described in this Proclamation; the East by the coast line, including the islands adjacent thereto; the West by the coast line, including the islands adjacent thereto; the South by the River Waitangi to its source, thence by a right line running to the source of the River Awarua, thence by the River Awarua to its mouth. The Province of *Otago* shall be bounded on the North by the southern boundary of the Province of Canterbury, as already described in this Proclamation; the East by the coast line, including the islands adjacent thereto; the West by the coast line, including the islands adjacent thereto; the South by the coast line, including the islands adjacent thereto, with the exception of Stewart's Island, its adjacent islands, and Sclanders Island, and the Island of Ruapuke." "The *Sic in Gazette, probably a misprint for "Solander."* Boundaries of Provinces Act, 1858," provides a machinery for settling disputes concerning boundaries. In addition to the above, the following Provinces have been established under "The New Provinces Act, 1858":—Hawke's Bay, on 1st November, 1858; Marlborough, on 1st November, 1859; and Southland, on 1st April, 1861. Westland was established by "The County of Westland Act, 1867."

([1]) So much of this section as relates to the signification of the disallowance by the Governor of any election of a Superintendent is repealed by "The Superintendents Election Disallowance Signification Act, 1866;" and a Proclamation in the *New Zealand Gazette* is substituted.

([2]) As to the causes by which the office of Superintendent may become vacant, see "The Disqualification Act, 1858," and "The Public Offenders' Disqualification Act, 1867."

signed by the majority of the Members of such Provincial Council praying for such removal; and thereupon the like proceedings shall be had as in the case of any such vacancy as above mentioned.

Governor may appoint electoral districts, &c.

5. It shall be lawful for the Governor, by Proclamation to constitute within each of the said Provinces hereby established convenient electoral districts for the election of Members of the Provincial Council, and of the Superintendent, and to appoint and declare the number of Members to be elected for each such district for the Provincial Council, and to make provision for the registration and revision of lists of all persons qualified to vote at the elections to be holden within such districts, and for the appointing of Returning Officers, and for issuing, executing, and returning the necessary writs for such elections, and for taking the poll thereat, and for determining the validity of all disputed returns, and otherwise for ensuring the orderly, effective, and impartial conduct of such elections; and in determining the number and extent of such electoral districts, and the number of Members to be elected for each district, regard shall be had to the number of electors within the same, so that the number of Members to be assigned to any one district may bear to the whole number of the Members of the said Council, as nearly as may be, the same proportion as the number of electors within such district shall bear to the whole number of electors within the limits of the Province.

Qualification of Members.

6. Every person within any Province hereby established, or hereafter to be established, who shall be legally qualified as an elector, and duly registered as such, shall be qualified to be elected a Member of the Provincial Council thereof, or to be elected Superintendent thereof: Provided always, that it shall not be necessary that he reside or possess the qualification in the particular district for which he may be elected to serve as a Member.

Qualification of voters.

7. The Members of every such Council shall be chosen by the votes of the inhabitants of the Province who may be qualified as hereinafter mentioned; that is to say, every man of the age of twenty-one years or upwards, having a freehold estate in possession, situate within the district for which the vote is to be given, of

the clear value of fifty pounds above all charges and incumbrances, and of or to which he has been seized or entitled, either at law or in equity, for at least six calendar months next before the last registration of the electors, or having a leasehold estate in possession, situate within such district, of the clear annual value of ten pounds, held upon a lease which at the time of such registration shall have not less than three years to run, or having a leasehold estate so situate, and of such value as aforesaid, of which he has been in possession for three years or upwards next before such registration, or being a householder within such district, occupying a tenement within the limits of a town (to be proclaimed as such by the Governor for the purposes of this Act), of the clear annual value of ten pounds, or without the limits of a town, of the clear annual value of five pounds, and having resided therein six calendar months next before such registration as aforesaid, shall, if duly registered, be entitled to vote at the election of a Member or Members for the district.

8. Provided always, that no person shall be entitled to vote at any such election who is an alien, or who at any time theretofore shall have been attainted or convicted of any treason, felony, or infamous offence, within any part of Her Majesty's dominions, unless he shall have received a free pardon, or shall have undergone the sentence or punishment to which he shall have been adjudged for such offence. *Aliens and persons convicted of certain offences disqualified.*

9. It shall be lawful for any Member of any Provincial Council, by writing under his hand, addressed to the Superintendent of the Province, to resign his seat in the said Council; and upon the receipt by the Superintendent of such resignation, the seat of such Member shall become vacant. *Members may resign their seats.*

10. If any Member of any Provincial Council shall, for two successive Sessions of such Council, fail to give his attendance therein, or shall become bankrupt, or shall become an insolvent debtor within the meaning of the laws relating to insolvent debtors, or shall become a public defaulter, or be attainted of treason, or be convicted of felony or any infamous offence, his seat in such Council shall thereupon become vacant.(¹) *In certain cases seats to become void.*

(¹) See note (2) to sec. 4.

Determination of questions as to vacancies.

11. Any question which shall arise respecting any vacancy in a Provincial Council on occasion of any of the matters aforesaid shall be heard and determined by such Council, on such question being referred to them for that purpose by the Superintendent of the Province, and not otherwise.[1]

Issue of writs for supplying vacancies.

12. Whenever it shall be established to the satisfaction of the Superintendent, that the seat of any Member of the Provincial Council has become vacant, the Superintendent shall forthwith issue a writ for the election of a new Member to serve in the place so vacated, during the remainder of the term of the continuance of such Council, and no longer.[2]

Duration of Provincial Council.

13. Every Provincial Council shall continue for the period of four years from the day of the return of the writs for choosing the same, and no longer: Provided

Dissolution.

always, that it shall be lawful for the Governor, by Proclamation or otherwise, sooner to dissolve the same, whenever he shall deem it expedient so to do.

When writs are to issue.

14. The Governor shall cause the first writs for the election of Members of the Provincial Council of every Province hereby established to be issued at some time not later than six calendar months next after the proclamation of this Act in New Zealand; and upon the expiration of the said period of the continuance of any Provincial Council, or upon the previous dissolution thereof, the Governor shall cause writs to be issued for the election of Members of the ensuing Council.

Convening of Council.

15. It shall be lawful for the Superintendent, by Proclamation in the Government *Gazette*, to fix such place or places within the limits of the Province, and such times for holding the first and every other session of the Provincial Council, as he may think fit, and from time to time, in manner aforesaid, to alter and vary such times and places as he may judge advisable, and most consistent with general convenience.

Prorogation.

16. It shall be lawful for the Superintendent to prorogue such Council from time to time, whenever he shall deem it expedient so to do.

---

[1] Other questions of vacancy may be determined on information in the nature of a *quo warranto*. See " Provincial Elections Act, 1858," sec. 9.

[2] See " The Provincial Elections Act, 1858," sec. 7.

17. Provided always, that there shall be a session of every Provincial Council once at least in every year, so that a greater period than twelve calendar months shall not intervene between the last sitting of the Council in one session, and the first sitting of the Council in the next session. *A session to be held every year.*

18. It shall be lawful for the Superintendent of each Province, with the advice and consent of the Provincial Council thereof, to make and ordain all such laws and ordinances (except and subject as hereinafter mentioned) as may be required for the peace, order, and good government of such Province, provided that the same be not repugnant to the law of England. (¹) *Superintendent and Provincial Council may make laws.*

19. It shall not be lawful for the Superintendent and Provincial Council to make or ordain any law or ordinance for any of the purposes hereinafter mentioned; (²) (that is to say)— *Restrictions on powers of legislation.*

(1.)• The imposition or regulation of Duties of Customs to be imposed on the importation or exportation of any goods at any port or place in the Province :

(2.) The establishment or abolition of any Court of judicature of civil or criminal jurisdiction, except Courts for trying and punishing such offences as by the law of New Zealand are or may be made punishable in a summary way, or altering the constitution, jurisdiction, or practice of any such Court except as aforesaid : (³)

(3.) Regulating any of the current coin, or the issue of any bills, notes, or other paper currency :

(4.) Regulating the weights and measures to be used in the Province, or in any part thereof :

(5.) Regulating the post offices and the carriage of letters within the Province :

(¹) Doubts as to the powers of Provincial Councils to authorize the compulsory taking of private land, and to create corporations, are set at rest by the Provincial Compulsory Land Taking Acts 1863 and 1866, and by " The Provincial Corporations Act, 1865."

(²) See sec. 53, *post,* which makes Provincial Acts, so far as repugnant to any Act of the General Assembly, void.

(³) See " The Provincial Councils' Powers Act, 1856," which gives Provincial Legislatures power to alter the civil jurisdiction of Courts of summary procedure, where the debt or damage claimed shall not exceed £20.

2

(6.) Establishing, altering, or repealing laws relating to bankruptcy or insolvency:

(7.) The erection and maintenance of beacons and
lighthouses on the coast:

(8.) The imposition of any dues or other charges on
shipping at any port or harbour in the Province :

(9.) Regulating marriages :

(10.) Affecting lands of the Crown, or lands to
which the title of the aboriginal native owners
has never been extinguished :(¹)

(11.) Inflicting any disabilities or restrictions on
persons of the Native races to which persons
of European birth or descent would not also
be subjected :

(12.) Altering in any way the criminal law of New
Zealand, except so far as relates to the trial
and punishment of such offences as are now
or may, by the criminal law of New Zealand,
be punishable in a summary way, as aforesaid :(²)

(13.) Regulating the course of inheritance of real or
personal property, or affecting the law relating to wills.

As to election of Speaker. 20. Every Provincial Council shall, immediately on their first meeting, and before proceeding to the despatch of any other business, elect one of their Members to be the Speaker thereof during the continuance of such Council, which election being confirmed by the Super-intendent, shall be valid and effectual ; and in case of vacancy in the said office by death, resignation, or other-wise, then and so often as the same shall happen, the election shall be repeated and confirmed as aforesaid.

Speaker to preside. 21. The Speaker of each Provincial Council shall preside at the meetings of such Council; but in his

---

(¹) See "The Highways and Watercourses Diversion Act, 1858 ;" "The Provincial Councils' Powers Extension Act, 1863 ;" and "The Provincial Councils' Powers Extension Act, 1865," which give Pro-vincial Legislatures power to deal with public roads and the beds of watercourses though the soil is vested in the Crown.

(²) By "The Provincial Councils' Powers Act, 1856," Provincial Legislatures may create offences under the degree of felony, punishable with not more than six months' imprisonment with hard labour, or a penalty of £100.

absence, some Member elected by the Council shall preside.

22. No Provincial Council shall be competent to the despatch of any business, unless one-third of the whole number of Members be present. *Quorum.*

23. All questions which shall arise in any such Council shall be decided by the majority of votes of the Members present other than the Speaker or presiding Member; but, in all cases wherein the votes shall be equal, the Speaker or presiding Member shall have a casting vote. *Questions to be determined by majority of votes.*

24. Every Provincial Council, at their first meeting, and from time to time afterwards, as occasion may require, shall prepare and adopt such standing rules and orders as may be best adapted for the orderly conduct of the business of such Council, which rules and orders shall be laid before the Superintendent; and, being by him approved, shall then become binding and in force. *Standing orders to be adopted.*

25. It shall not be lawful for any Provincial Council to pass, or for the Superintendent to assent to, any Bill appropriating any money to the public service, unless the Superintendent shall first have recommended to the Council to make provision for the specific service to which such money is to be appropriated; and no such money shall be issued, or be made issuable, except by warrants to be granted by the Superintendent. *Appropriation and issue of money.*

26. It shall be lawful for the Superintendent to transmit to the Provincial Council, for their consideration, the drafts of any such laws or ordinances as it may appear to him desirable to introduce; and all such drafts shall be taken into consideration in such convenient manner as in and by such rules and orders as aforesaid shall be in that behalf provided. *Superintendent may transmit drafts of laws for consideration of Council.*

27. Every Bill passed by the Provincial Council shall be presented to the Superintendent for the Governor's assent; and the Superintendent shall declare, according to his discretion (but subject, nevertheless, to the provisions herein contained, and to such instructions as may from time to time be given him by the Governor), that he assents to such Bill on behalf of the Governor, or that he withholds the assent of the Governor, or that he reserves such Bill for the signification of the Governor's pleasure thereon: Provided always, that it shall and *Giving or withholding assent to Bills.*

may be lawful for the Superintendent, before declaring his pleasure in regard to any Bill so presented to him, to make such amendments in such Bill as he thinks needful or expedient, and to return such Bill with such amendments to such Council, and the consideration of such amendments by such Council shall take place in such convenient manner as shall, in and by the rules and orders aforesaid, be in that behalf provided : Provided also, that all Bills altering or affecting the extent of the several electoral districts which shall be represented in the Provincial Council, or establishing new or other such electoral districts, or altering the number of the Members of such Council to be chosen by the said districts respectively, or altering the number of the Members of such Council, or altering the limits of any town, or establishing any new town, shall be so reserved as aforesaid.

Superintendent to send copies of Bills assented to to Governor. 28. Whenever any Bill shall have been assented to by the Superintendent as aforesaid, the Superintendent shall forthwith transmit to the Governor an authentic copy thereof.

Disallowance of Bills assented to. 29. It shall be lawful for the Governor, at any time within three months after any such Bill shall have been received by him, to declare, by Proclamation, his disallowance of such Bill; and such disallowance shall make void and annul the same, from and after the day of the date of such Proclamation, or any subsequent day to be named therein.

No Bill to have any force until assented to by Governor. 30. (¹)No Bill which shall be reserved for the signification of the assent of the Governor shall have any force and authority within the Province until the Superintendent shall signify, either by speech or message to the Provincial Council, or by Proclamation in the Government *Gazette*, that such Bill has been laid before the Governor, and that the Governor has assented to the same ; and an entry shall be made in the journals of the Provincial Council of every such speech, message, or Proclamation ; and a duplicate thereof, duly attested,

---

(¹) This section is repealed by "The Provincial Reserved Bills Act, 1858," and substantially re-enacted with this difference, that the three months run from the day on which the Bill is received by the Governor, not from the day on which it is presented to the Superintendent. Under this Act the Proclamation must be in the Government *Gazette* of the Province.

shall be delivered to the Registrar of the Supreme Court, or other proper officer, to be kept among the records of the Province; and no Bill which shall be so reserved, as aforesaid, shall have any force or authority within the Province, unless the assent of the Governor thereto shall have been so signified, as aforesaid, within three months next after the day on which such Bill shall have been presented to the Superintendent for the Governor's assent.

31. It shall be lawful for the Governor, from time to time, to transmit to the Superintendent of any Province, for his guidance in assenting to or withholding assent from bills, or reserving the same for the signification of the Governor's pleasure thereon, such instructions as to the Governor shall seem fit; and it shall be the duty of the Superintendent to act in obedience to such instructions. *Governor may transmit instructions to Superintendent as to reserving Bills.*

32. There shall be within the Colony of New Zealand a General Assembly, to consist of the Governor, a Legislative Council, and House of Representatives. *Establishment of a General Assembly.*

33. For constituting the Legislative Council of New Zealand, it shall be lawful for Her Majesty, before the time to be appointed for the first meeting of the General Assembly, by an instrument under her Royal Sign Manual, to authorize the Governor, in Her Majesty's name, to summon to the said Legislative Council such persons, being not less in number than ten, as Her Majesty shall think fit; and it shall also be lawful for Her Majesty, from time to time, in like manner to authorize the Governor to summon to the said Legislative Council such other person or persons as Her Majesty shall think fit, either for supplying any vacancy or vacancies or otherwise; and every person who shall be so summoned shall thereby become a Member of the said Legislative Council:(¹) Provided always, that no person shall be summoned to such Legislative Council who shall not be of the full age of twenty-one years, and a natural-born subject of *Appointment of Members of the Legislative Council.*

(¹) Doubts having arisen as to the necessity for Members of the Legislative Council being approved of by Her Majesty before being summoned, the Imperial Act 31 and 32 Vict. cap. 57, (proclaimed in New Zealand on 29th January, 1869,) *post*, was passed, giving the future selection of Members to the Governor, and confirming all previous appointments.

Her Majesty, or a subject of Her Majesty naturalized by Act of Parliament, or by an Act of the Legislature of New Zealand.

Legislative Councillors may hold seats for life. 34. Every Member of the Legislative Council of New Zealand shall hold his seat therein for the term of his life; subject, nevertheless, to the provisions hereinafter contained for vacating the same.

Resignation of seat in Council. 35. It shall be lawful for any Member of the said Legislative Council, by writing under his hand, addressed to the Governor, to resign his seat in the said Council; and upon such resignation and acceptance thereof by the Governor, the seat of such Member shall become vacant.

Causes by which seat may be vacated. 36. If any Legislative Councillor of New Zealand shall, for two successive sessions of the General Assembly, without the permission of Her Majesty or of the Governor, signified by the said Governor to the Legislative Council, fail to give his attendance in the said Legislative Council, or shall take any oath, or make any declaration or acknowledgment of allegiance, obedience, or adherence to any foreign Prince or Power, or shall do, concur in, or adopt any act whereby he may become a subject or citizen of any foreign State or Power, or become entitled to the rights, privileges, or immunities, of a subject or citizen of any foreign State or Power, or shall become bankrupt, or shall become an insolvent debtor, within the meaning of the laws relating to insolvent debtors, or shall become a public defaulter, or be attainted of treason, or be convicted of felony, or any infamous crime, his seat in such . Council shall thereby become vacant.[1]

Trial of question whether seats are vacated. 37. Any question which shall arise respecting any vacancy in the said Legislative Council, on occasion of any of the matters aforesaid, shall be referred by the Governor to the said Legislative Council, to be by the said Legislative Council heard and determined : Provided always, that it shall be lawful, either for the person respecting whose seat such question shall have arisen, or for Her Majesty's Attorney-General for New Zealand on Her Majesty's behalf, to appeal from the

---

[1] See " The Public Offenders' Disqualification Act, 1867," for some further causes by which the seat of a Legislative Councillor may become vacant.

determination of the said Council in such case to Her Majesty; and the judgment of Her Majesty, given with the advice of Her Privy Council thereon, shall be final and conclusive to all intents and purposes.

38. The Governor shall have power and authority from time to time to appoint one Member of the said Legislative Council to be Speaker of such Council, and to remove him and appoint another in his stead. *Appointment of Speaker of Legislative Council.*

39. The presence of at least five Members of the said Legislative Council, including the Speaker, shall be necessary to constitute a meeting for the exercise of its powers;(¹) and all questions which shall arise in the said Legislative Council shall be decided by a majority of votes of the Members present other than the Speaker, and when the votes shall be equal, the Speaker shall have the casting vote. *Quorum, &c.*

40. For the purpose of constituting the House of Representatives of New Zealand, it shall be lawful for the Governor, within the time hereinafter mentioned, and thereafter from time to time as occasion shall require, by Proclamation in Her Majesty's name, to summon and call together a House of Representatives in and for New Zealand, such House of Representatives to consist of such number of Members not more than forty-two nor less than twenty-four, as the Governor shall by Proclamation in that behalf direct and appoint;(²) and every such House of Representatives shall, unless the General Assembly shall be sooner dissolved, continue for the period of five years from the day of the return of the writs for choosing such House, and no longer. *Power to summon a House of Representatives by Proclamation in Her Majesty's name.*

41. It shall be lawful for the Governor, by Proclamation, to constitute within New Zealand convenient *Power to Governor by Proclamation to constitute electoral districts, &c., for election of Members of House of Representatives.*

(¹) So much of this section as fixes the number necessary to constitute a quorum, is repealed by "The Legislative Council Quorum Act, 1865," which enacts that the number shall be regulated by the Council.

(²) By Proclamation of 5th March, 1853, the number of Members of the House of Representatives was fixed at thirty-seven. It has since been increased as follows:—By "The Electoral Districts Act, 1858," to 41. By "The Representation Act, 1860," to 53. By "The Representation Act, 1862," to 57. By "The Representation Act, 1865," to 70. By "The Westland Representation Act, 1867," to 72. By "The Maori Representation Act, 1867," four additional members are given, to be elected by Maoris. This Act continues for five years from 10th October, 1867.

electoral districts for the election of Members of the said House of Representatives, and to appoint and declare the number of such Members to be elected for each such district, and to make provision (so far as may be necessary beyond the provision which may be made for the like purposes in relation to elections for Provincial Councils) for the registration and revision of lists of all persons qualified to vote at the elections to be holden within such districts, and also provision for the appointing of Returning Officers, and for issuing, executing, and returning the necessary writs for elections of Members of the House of Representatives, and for taking the poll thereat, and otherwise for ensuring the orderly, effective, and impartial conduct of such elections; and in determining the number and extent of such electoral districts, and the number of Members to be elected for each district, regard shall be had to the number of electors within the same, so that the number of Members to be assigned to any one district may bear to the whole number of the Members of the House of Representatives, as nearly as may be, the same proportion as the number of electors within such district shall bear to the whole number of electors in New Zealand.([1])

Qualification of voters for Members of House of Representatives. 42. The Members of the said House of Representatives to be chosen in every electoral district appointed for that purpose, shall be chosen by the votes of the inhabitants of New Zealand who shall possess within such district the like qualifications which, when possessed within an electoral district appointed for the election of Members of the Provincial Council, would entitle inhabitants of the Province to vote in the election of Members of the Provincial Council thereof, and who shall be duly registered as electors; and every person legally qualified as such elector shall be qualified to be elected a Member of the said House.([2])

First writs to be issued within six months. 43. The Governor shall cause the first writs for the election of Members of the said House of Representatives to be issued at some time not later than six calendar months next after the proclamation of this Act in New Zealand; and upon the expiration of the said

---

([1]) See the Acts mentioned in note to sec. 40.
([2]) As to qualification, see the Miners' Representation Acts.

/

period of the continuance of the House of Representatives, or upon the previous determination of such House by the dissolution of the General Assembly, the Governor shall cause writs to be issued for the election of Members of the ensuing House of Representatives.

44. The General Assembly of New Zealand shall be holden at any place and time within New Zealand which the Governor shall from time to time by Proclamation for that purpose appoint; and the time so to be appointed for the first holding of such General Assembly shall be as soon as conveniently may be after the return of the first writs for the election of Members of the said House of Representatives; and the Governor may, at his pleasure, prorogue or dissolve the General Assembly. *Time and place of holding the General Assembly. Prorogation and dissolution.*

45. The said House of Representatives shall, until provision be made otherwise in that behalf by law, be judges, without appeal, of the validity of the election of each Member thereof. *Disputed elections.*

46. No Member of the said Legislative Council or House of Representatives shall be permitted to sit or vote therein until he shall have taken and subscribed the following oath before the Governor, or before some person or persons authorized by him to administer such oath :— *No Member to sit or vote until he has taken the oath of allegiance.*

" I, A.B., do sincerely promise and swear that I will be faithful, and bear true allegiance to Her Majesty Queen Victoria. So help me God." *Oath of allegiance.*

47. Every person authorized by law to make his solemn affirmation or declaration, instead of taking an oath, may make such affirmation or declaration in lieu of the said oath. *Affirmation or declaration in lieu of oath.*

48. The said House of Representatives shall, immediately on their first meeting, proceed to the choice of one of their Members as their Speaker during the continuance of the said House, which choice, being confirmed by the Governor, shall be valid and effectual; and in case of vacancy of the office by death, resignation, or otherwise, then and so often as the same shall happen, the choice shall be repeated and confirmed as aforesaid. *Speaker to be elected on first meeting of House of Representatives.*

49. It shall be lawful for any Member of the said House of Representatives, by writing under his hand *Resignation of seats.*

3

addressed to the Speaker of the said House, to resign his seat in the said House, and upon such resignation the seat of such Member shall become vacant.

Vacating of seats in certain cases.

50. If any Member of the said House of Representatives shall, for one whole session of the General Assembly, without the permission of such House, fail to give his attendance in the said House, or shall take any oath, or make any declaration or acknowledgment of allegiance, obedience, or adherence, to any foreign Prince or Power, or do, or concur in, or adopt any act whereby he may become a subject or citizen of any foreign State or Power, or become entitled to the rights, privileges, or immunities of a subject of any foreign State or Power, or shall become bankrupt, or shall become an insolvent debtor within the meaning of the laws relating to insolvent debtors, or shall become a public defaulter, or be attainted of treason, or be convicted of felony or any infamous crime, his seat in such House shall thereby become vacant.(¹)

Election to take place on vacancies.

51. When and so often as a vacancy shall occur as aforesaid in any seat in the said House of Representatives, it shall and may be lawful for such House to address the Governor, stating the existence of such vacancy, and the cause thereof; and the Governor, upon receiving such address, shall cause a writ to be issued for supplying such vacancy.(²)

Standing rules and orders to be made.

52. (³)The said Legislative Council and House of Representatives, at the first sitting of each respectively, and from time to time afterwards as there shall be occasion, shall prepare and adopt such standing rules and orders as shall appear to the said Council and House of Representatives respectively best adapted for the orderly conduct of the business of such Council and House respectively, and for the manner in which such Council and House respectively shall be presided over in case of the absence of the Speaker, and for the mode in which such Council and House shall confer, correspond, and communicate with each other relative to votes or Bills passed by or pending in such Council

---

(¹) See " The Disqualification Act, 1858," and " The Public Offenders' Disqualification Act, 1867."

(²) See "The Elections Writs Act, 1858," as to vacancies in recess.

(³) Repealed by " The Parliamentary Privileges Act, 1865."

and House respectively, and for the manner in which notices of Bills, Resolutions, and other business intended to be submitted to such Council and House respectively at any session thereof, may be published in the Government *Gazette*, or otherwise, for general information, for some convenient space or time before the meeting of such Council and House respectively, and for the proper framing, entitling, and numbering of the Bills to be introduced into and passed by the said Council and House of Representatives, all of which rules and orders shall by such Council and House respectively be laid before the Governor, and being by him approved, shall become binding and of force; but subject, nevertheless, to the confirmation or disallowance of Her Majesty in manner hereinafter provided respecting the acts to be made by the Governor, with the advice and consent of the said Legislative Council and House of Representatives : Provided, that no such rule or order shall be of force to subject any person, not being a Member or Officer of the Council or House to which it relates, to any pain, penalty, or forfeiture.

53. It shall be competent to the said General Assembly (except and subject as hereinafter mentioned) to make laws for the peace, order, and good government of New Zealand, provided that no such laws be repugnant to the law of England; and the laws so to be made by the said General Assembly shall control and supersede any laws or ordinances in anywise repugnant thereto, which may have been made or ordained prior thereto by any Provincial Council; and any law or ordinance made or ordained by any Provincial Council, in pursuance of the authority hereby conferred upon it, and on any subject whereon, under such authority as aforesaid, it is entitled to legislate, shall, so far as the same is repugnant to, or inconsistent with, any Act passed by the General Assembly, be null and void. *Power of General Assembly to make laws.*

54. It shall not be lawful for the House of Representatives or the Legislative Council to pass, or for the Governor to assent to, any Bill appropriating to the public service any sum of money from or out of Her Majesty's revenue within New Zealand, unless the Governor, on Her Majesty's behalf, shall first have recommended to the House of Representatives to make *As to the appropriation and issue of money.*

provision for the specific public service towards which such money is to be appropriated, and (save as herein otherwise provided) no part of Her Majesty's revenue within New Zealand shall be issued, except in pursuance of warrants under the hand of the Governor, directed to the public Treasurer thereof.

Governor may transmit drafts of laws to either House.
55. It shall and may be lawful for the Governor to transmit by message to either the said Legislative Council or the said House of Representatives, for their consideration, the drafts of any laws which it may appear to him desirable to introduce, and all such drafts shall be taken into consideration in such convenient manner as shall, in and by the rules and orders aforesaid, be in that behalf provided.

Governor may assent to, refuse assent, or reserve Bills.
56. Whenever any Bill which has been passed by the said Legislative Council and House of Representatives shall be presented for Her Majesty's assent to the Governor, he shall declare according to his discretion, but subject, nevertheless, to the provisions contained in this Act, and to such instructions as may from time to time be given in that behalf by Her Majesty, her heirs or successors, that he assents to such Bill in Her Majesty's name, or that he refuses his assent to such Bill, or that he reserves such Bill for the signification of Her Majesty's pleasure thereon : Provided always, that it shall and may be lawful for the Governor, before declaring his pleasure in regard to any Bill so presented to him, to make such amendments in such Bill as he thinks needful or expedient, and by message to return such Bill with such amendments to the Legislative Council or the House of Representatives, as he shall think the more fitting, and the consideration of such amendments by the said Council and House respectively shall take place in such convenient manner as shall, in and by the rules and orders aforesaid, be in that behalf provided.

Governor to conform to instructions transmitted by Her Majesty.
57. It shall be lawful for Her Majesty, with the advice of Her Privy Council, or under Her Majesty's Signet and Sign Manual, or through one of her Principal Secretaries of State, from time to time to convey to the Governor of New Zealand such instructions as to Her Majesty shall seem meet, for the guidance of such Governor, for the exercise of the powers hereby vested

in him, of assenting to, or dissenting from, or for reserving for the signification of Her Majesty's pleasure, Bills to be passed by the said Legislative Council and House of Representatives; and it shall be the duty of such Governor to act in obedience to such instructions. (¹)

58. Whenever any Bill which shall have been presented for Her Majesty's assent to the Governor shall by such Governor have been assented to in Her Majesty's name, he shall, by the first convenient opportunity, transmit to one of Her Majesty's Principal Secretaries of State an authentic copy of such Bill so assented to; and it shall be lawful, at any time within two years after such Bill shall have been received by the Secretary of State, for Her Majesty, by Order in Council, to declare her disallowance of such Bill; and such disallowance, together with a certificate under the hand and seal of the Secretary of State, certifying the day on which such Bill was received as aforesaid, being signified by the Governor to the said Legislative Council and House of Representatives by speech or message, or by proclamation in the Government *Gazette,* shall make void and annul the same, from and after the day of such signification. *[marginal note: As to disallowance by Her Majesty of Bills assented to by the Governor.]*

59. No Bill which shall be reserved for the signification of Her Majesty's pleasure thereon shall have any force or authority within New Zealand until the Governor shall signify, either by speech or message to the said Legislative Council and House of Representatives, or by Proclamation, that such Bill has been laid before Her Majesty in Council, and that Her *[marginal note: No reserved Bill to have any force until assented to by Her Majesty.]*

(¹) By the instructions of 14th November, 1867, to Sir G. F. Bowen, the following classes of Bills are directed to be reserved for the signification of Her Majesty's pleasure, except in cases of urgent necessity :—

1. Divorce Bills.
2. Bills making a grant to the Governor.
3. Bills making paper or other currency (except coin of the realm, or gold or silver coin,) a legal tender.
4. Bills imposing differential duties.
5. Bills inconsistent with Imperial treaties.
6. Bills interfering with discipline or control of Her Majesty's forces.
7. Bills of an extraordinary nature prejudicial to the Royal prerogative, rights of non-resident subjects, or trade and shipping of the United Kindom or its dependencies.
8. Bills containing provisions once disallowed or to which Royal assent has been refused.

Majesty has been pleased to assent to the same; and an entry shall be made in the Journals of the said Legislative Council and House of Representatives of every such speech, message, or proclamation, and a duplicate thereof, duly attested, shall be delivered to the Registrar of the Supreme Court, or other proper officer, to be kept among the records of New Zealand; and no Bill which shall be so reserved as aforesaid shall have any force or authority within New Zealand, unless Her Majesty's assent thereto shall have been so signified as aforesaid within the space of two years from the day on which such Bill shall have been presented for Her Majesty's assent to the Governor as aforesaid.

Acts to be printed.

60. The Governor shall cause every Act of the said General Assembly which he shall have assented to in Her Majesty's name to be printed in the Government *Gazette* for general information, and such publication by such Governor of any such Act shall be deemed to be in law the promulgation of the same.

Duties not to be levied on supplies for troops, nor any dues, &c., inconsistent with treaties.

61. It shall not be lawful for the said General Assembly to levy any duty upon articles imported for the supply of Her Majesty's land or sea forces, or to levy any duty, impose any prohibition or restriction, or grant any exemptions, bounty, drawback, or other privilege upon the importation or exportation of any articles, or to impose any dues or charges upon shipping contrary to, or at variance with, any treaty or treaties concluded by Her Majesty with any foreign Power.

Expenses of collection of revenue.

62. (¹)The Governor is hereby authorized and required to pay, out of the revenue arising from taxes, duties, rates, and imposts, levied under any Act or Acts of the said General Assembly, and from the disposal of waste lands of the Crown, all the costs, charges, and expenses incident to the collection, management, and receipt thereof; also to pay out of the said revenue arising from the disposal of waste lands of the Crown such sums as may become payable under the provisions hereinafter contained, for or on account of the purchase of land from aboriginal natives or the release or extinguishment of their rights in any land, and such

(¹) Partly repealed by "The Ordinary Revenue Act, 1858," and partly repealed by 20 and 21 Vict. c. 53 (Imperial), *post.*

sums as may become payable to the New Zealand Company under the provisions of this Act in respect of the sale or alienation of land : Provided always, that full and particular accounts of all such disbursements shall from time to time be laid before the said Legislative Council and House of Representatives.

63. (¹) All costs, charges, and expenses, of or incident to the collection, management, and receipt of duties of import and export shall be regulated and audited in such manner as shall be directed by the Commissioners of Her Majesty's Treasury of the United Kingdom of Great Britain and Ireland ; and all such costs, charges, and expenses in relation to other branches of the said revenue shall be regulated and audited in such manner as shall be directed by laws of the said General Assembly. *Audit of accounts.*

64. There shall be payable to Her Majesty, every year, out of the revenue arising from such taxes, duties, rates, and imposts, and from the disposal of such waste lands of the Crown in New Zealand, the several sums mentioned in the schedule to this Act ; (²) such several sums to be paid for defraying the expenses of the services and purposes mentioned in such schedule, and to be issued by the Treasurer of New Zealand in discharge of such warrants as shall be from time to time directed to him under the hand and seal of the Governor ; and the said Treasurer shall account to Her Majesty for the same through the Commissioners of Her Majesty's Treasury of the United Kingdom of Great Britain and Ireland, in such manner and form as Her Majesty shall be graciously pleased to direct. *Grants for civil and judicial services.*

65. It shall be lawful for the General Assembly of New Zealand, by any Act or Acts, to alter all or any of the sums mentioned in the said schedule, and the appropriation of such sums to the services and purposes therein mentioned ; but every Bill which shall be passed by the said Legislative Council and House of Represen- *How the appropriation of sums granted may be varied.*

(¹) Repealed by "The Ordinary Revenue Act, 1858."

(¹) The Civil List has been altered successively by "The Governors Salary Act, 1856," and the Civil List Acts of 1858, 1862, 1863, under the powers given by sec. 65 of the Constitution Act. There was also a temporary addition made to the moneys applicable to Native purposes by "The Native Purposes Appropriation Act, 1862." The latter part of this section was repealed by "The Surplus Revenues Act, 1858."

tatives altering the salary of the Governor, or altering
the sum described as for Native purposes, shall be
reserved for the signification of Her Majesty's pleasure
thereon, and until and subject to such alteration by Act
or Acts as aforesaid, the salaries of the Governor and
Judges shall be those respectively set against their
several offices in the said schedule; and accounts in
detail of the expenditure of the several sums for the
time being appropriated under this Act, or such Act or
Acts as aforesaid of the said General Assembly, to the
several services and purposes mentioned in the said
schedule, shall be laid before the said Legislative
Council and House of Representatives within thirty
days next after the beginning of the Session after such
expenditure shall have been made : Provided always,
that it shall not be lawful for the said General Assembly,
by any such Act as aforesaid, to make any diminution
in the salary of any Judge, to take effect during the
continuance in office of any person being such Judge at
the time of the passing of such Act.

Appropriation of revenue. 66. (¹)After and subject to the payments to be made
under the provisions hereinbefore contained, all the
revenue arising from taxes, duties, rates, and imposts
levied in virtue of any Act of the General Assembly,
and from the disposal of waste lands of the Crown,
under any such Act made in pursuance of the authority
herein contained, shall be subject to be appropriated to
such specific purposes as by any Act of the said General
Assembly shall be prescribed in that behalf; and the
surplus of such revenue which shall not be appropriated as aforesaid, shall be divided among the several '
Provinces for the time being established in New
Zealand under or by virtue of this Act, in the like proportion as the gross proceeds of the said revenue shall
have arisen therein respectively, and shall be paid over
to the respective Treasuries of such Provinces for the
public uses thereof, and shall be subject to the appro-

(¹) Repeated changes have been made in the mode of appropriating
revenue by the following Acts :—(1.) As to Surplus Revenue : by
"The Surplus Revenues Act, 1858," and "The Public Revenues Act,
1867." (2.) As to Land Revenue: by "The Land Revenue Appropriation Act, 1858," "The Land Revenue Appropriation Act Amendment Act (No. 1), 1862," "The Land Revenue Appropriation Act
Amendment Act (No. 2), 1862," and "The Public Revenues Act, 1867."

priation of the respective Provincial Councils of such Provinces.

67. (¹)It shall be lawful for the said General Assembly, by any Act or Acts, from time to time, to establish new electoral districts for the purpose of electing Members of the said House of Representatives, to alter the boundaries of electoral districts for the time being existing for such purposes, to alter and appoint the number of Members to be chosen for such districts, to increase the whole number of Members of the said House of Representatives, and to alter and regulate the appointment of Returning Officers, and make provision in such manner as they may deem expedient for the issue and return of writs for the election of the Members of such House, and the time and place of holding such elections, and for the determination of contested elections for such House.

Power to General Assembly to alter electoral districts and number of Members of House of Representatives.

68. (¹)It shall be lawful for the said General Assembly, by any Act or Acts, to alter from time to time any provisions of this Act, and any laws for the time being in force concerning the election of Members of the said House of Representatives, and the qualification of electors and Members : Provided, that every Bill for any of such purposes shall be reserved for the signification of Her Majesty's pleasure thereon, and a copy of such Bill shall be laid before both Houses of Parliament for the space of thirty days at the least before Her Majesty's pleasure thereon shall be signified.

Power to General Assembly to make other alterations in the constitution of the House of Representatives.

69. (²) It shall be lawful for the said General Assembly, by any Act or Acts, from time to time, to constitute new Provinces in New Zealand, to direct and appoint the number of Members of which the Provincial Councils thereof shall consist, and to alter the boundaries of any Provinces for the time being existing, and to alter the provisions of this Act, and any laws for the time being in force respecting the election of Members of the Provincial Councils, the powers of such Councils, and the distribution of the said surplus revenue between the several Provinces of New Zealand :

Power to General Assembly to constitute Provinces, and alter the provisions concerning election of Members, &c.

(¹) These sections are repealed by the Imperial Act 20 and 21 Vict. c. 53, *post.*

(²) *Vide* sections 67 and 68.

(¹) Provided always, that any Bill for any of the said purposes shall be reserved for the signification of Her Majesty's pleasure thereon.

Her Majesty may establish Municipal Corporations.

70. It shall be lawful for Her Majesty, in and by any Letters Patent to be issued under the Great Seal of the United Kingdom, from time to time, to constitute and establish within any district or districts of New Zealand one or more Municipal Corporation or Corporations, and to grant to any such Corporation all or any of the powers which, in pursuance of the Statutes in that behalf made and provided, it is competent to Her Majesty to grant to the inhabitants of any town or borough in England and Wales incorporated in virtue of such Statutes or any of them, and to qualify and restrict the exercise of any such powers in such and the same manner as by the Statutes aforesaid, or any of them, Her Majesty may qualify or restrict the exercise of any such powers as aforesaid in England : Provided always, that all provisions of any such Letters Patent, and all bye-laws or regulations made by any such Corporation, shall be subject to alteration or repeal by any Ordinance or Act of the Provincial Council for the Province in which any such Corporation may be established, or of the General Assembly, according to their respective powers hereinbefore declared.

Her Majesty may cause laws of Aboriginal Native inhabitants to be maintained.

71. And whereas it may be expedient that the laws, customs, and usages of the Aboriginal or Native inhabitants of New Zealand, so far as they are not repugnant to the general principles of humanity, should for the present be maintained for the government of themselves in all their relations to and dealings with each other, and that particular districts should be set apart within which such laws, customs, or usages should be so observed :

It shall be lawful for Her Majesty, by any Letters Patent to be issued under the Great Seal of the United Kingdom, from time to time to make provision for the purposes aforesaid, any repugnancy of any such Native laws, customs, or usages to the law of England, or to any

---

(¹) See the New Provinces Acts referred to *ante*, p. 3, note (1). Also, "The County of Westland Act, 1868," and the Imperial Act 31 and 32 Vict., c. 92, declaring the powers of the General Assembly to withdraw territory from a Province and to constitute Counties.

law, statute, or usage in force in New Zealand, or in any part thereof, in anywise notwithstanding.

72. Subject to the provisions herein contained, it shall be lawful for the said General Assembly to make laws for regulating the sale, letting, disposal, and occupation of the waste lands of the Crown in New Zealand; and all lands wherein the title of Natives shall be extinguished as hereinafter mentioned, and all such other lands as are described in an Act of the Session holden in the tenth and eleventh years of Her Majesty, chapter one hundred and twelve, to promote Colonization in New Zealand, and to authorize a loan to the New Zealand Company, as demesne lands of the Crown, shall be deemed and taken to be waste lands of the Crown within the meaning of this Act: Provided always, that, subject to the said provisions, and until the said General Assembly shall otherwise enact, it shall be lawful for Her Majesty to regulate such sale, letting, disposal, and occupation, by instructions to be issued under the Signet and Royal Sign Manual.

Power to General Assembly to regulate sales of waste lands.

73. It shall not be lawful for any person other than Her Majesty, her heirs or successors, to purchase, or in anywise acquire or accept, from the Aboriginal Natives, land of or belonging to or used or occupied by them in common as tribes or communities, or to accept any release or extinguishment of the rights of such Aboriginal Natives in any such land as aforesaid; and no conveyance or transfer, or agreement for the conveyance or transfer, of any such land, either in perpetuity or for any term or period, either absolutely or conditionally, and either in property or by way of lease or occupancy, and no such release or extinguishment, as aforesaid, shall be of any validity or effect, unless the same be made to, or entered into with, and accepted by, Her Majesty, her heirs or successors :(1) Provided always, that it shall be lawful for Her Majesty, her heirs and successors, by instructions under the Signet and Royal

---

(1) But, by "The Native Lands Act, 1867," a Native may charge his land with money advanced for the purpose of paying the expenses of obtaining a certificate of title through the Native Land Court, though the Native title is not extinguished; and, by the Native Lands Acts 1865 and 1869, Natives may deal with land the title to which has been determined by the Native Land Court, though no Crown Grant has been issued at the date of the transaction.

Sign Manual, or signified through one of Her Majesty's Principal Secretaries of State, to delegate her powers of accepting such conveyances or agreements, releases or relinquishments, to the Governor of New Zealand, or the Superintendent of any Province within the limits of such Province, and to prescribe or regulate the terms on which such conveyances or agreements, releases or extinguishments, shall be accepted.

10 & 11 Vict.
c. 112.

74. (¹)And whereas, under and by virtue of the said last-mentioned Act, and of a notice given on the fourth day of July, one thousand eight hundred and fifty, by the New Zealand Company, in pursuance of such Act, the sum of two hundred and sixty-eight thousand three hundred and seventy pounds fifteen shillings, with interest after the yearly rate of three pounds ten shillings per centum upon the said sum, or so much thereof as shall from time to time remain unpaid, is charged upon and payable to the New Zealand Company out of the proceeds of the sales of the demesne lands of the Crown in New Zealand :

Upon all sales of waste lands one-fourth part of the sum to be paid to New Zealand Company till their debt is discharged.

In respect of all sales or other alienations of any waste lands of the Crown in New Zealand in fee-simple, or for any less estate or interest (except by way of license for occupation for pastoral purposes for any term of years not exceeding seven, and not containing any contract for the renewal of the same, or for a further estate, interest, or license, or by way of reservation of such lands as may be required for public roads or other internal communications, whether by land or water, or for the use or benefit of the aboriginal inhabitants of the country, or for purposes of military defence, or as the sites of places of public worship, schools, or other public buildings, or as places for the interment of the dead, or places for the recreation and amusement of the inhabitants of any town or village, or as the sites of public quays or landing-places on the sea coast or shores of navigable streams, or for any other purpose of public safety, convenience, health, or enjoyment), there shall be paid to the said New Zealand Company,

(¹) This section is repealed by the Imperial Act 20 and 21 Vict. c. 53, *post*. That Act, however, contains a proviso, that the repeal shall only take effect if, on or before the 5th day of April, 1858, certain sums be paid to the New Zealand Company.

towards the discharge of the principal sum and interest charged as aforesaid, in lieu of all and every other claim of the said Company in respect of the said sum, except where otherwise hereinafter provided, so long as the same or any part thereof respectively shall remain unpaid, one fourth part of the sum paid by the purchaser in respect of every such sale or alienation: Provided always, that it shall be lawful for the New Zealand Company, by any resolution of a majority of the proprietors of the said Company present at any meeting of such proprietors, and certified under the common seal of such Company, to release all or any part of the said lands from the moneys or payment charged thereon by the said Act, or this Act, or any part of such moneys or payment, either absolutely, or upon any terms or conditions, as such proprietors may think fit. *Power to New Zealand Company to release lands from payments, &c.*

75. It shall not be lawful for the said General Assembly to repeal or interfere with all or any of the provisions of an Act of the Session holden in the thirteenth and fourteenth years of Her Majesty, chapter seventy, intituled, "An Act empowering the Canterbury Association to dispose of certain Lands in New Zealand," or of an Act passed in the Session then next following, chapter eighty-four, to alter and amend the said first-mentioned Act : Provided always, that, on the expiration or sooner determination of the functions, powers, and authorities now vested in, or lawfully exercised by the said Association, the provisions of the present Act shall come into force as regards the lands to which the said Acts relate. *Saving as to Canterbury Settlement lands. 13 & 14 Vict. c. 70. 14 & 15 Vict. c. 84.*

76. It shall be lawful for the Canterbury Association, at any time after a Provincial Council shall have been constituted under this Act for the Province of Canterbury, to transfer to the said Council all such functions, powers, and authorities, and the said Council is hereby empowered to accept such transfer, upon such terms and conditions as shall be agreed upon between the said Council and the said Association : Provided always, that nothing contained in such terms and conditions shall interfere with the rights of Her Majesty, her heirs and successors, or of the New Zealand Company, respectively; and from and after such time as *Power to Canterbury Association to transfer their powers to the Provincial Council.*

shall be agreed upon between the said Council and the said Association, the said Council shall have and be entitled to exercise all the said functions, powers, and authorities.([1])

Saving as to Nelson Trust Fund.

14 & 15 Vict. c. 86.

77. Nothing in this Act, or in any Act, Law, or Ordinance to be made by the said General Assembly, or by any Provincial Assembly, shall affect or interfere with so much of an Act of the Session holden in the fourteenth and fifteenth years of Her Majesty, chapter eighty-six, intituled "An Act to regulate the affairs of certain Settlements established by the New Zealand Company in New Zealand," as relates to the administration of the funds for the public purposes of the Settlement of Nelson.

Power to Her Majesty to regulate the disposal of waste lands in Otago.

78. And whereas certain terms of purchase and pasturage of land in the Settlement of Otago had been issued by the New Zealand Company before the fourth day of July, one thousand eight hundred and fifty, and the said terms, or part of them, were in force on that day as contracts between the New Zealand Company and the Association of Lay Members of the Free Church of Scotland, commonly called the Otago Association : And whereas, by the provisions of the said Act of the tenth and eleventh years of Her Majesty, and of the said notice given by the New Zealand Company, the lands of the said Company in New Zealand reverted to and became vested in Her Majesty as part of the demesne lands of the Crown, subject nevertheless to any contract then subsisting in regard to any of the said lands : And whereas it is expedient that provision should be made to enable Her Majesty to fulfil the contracts contained in such terms of purchase and pasturage as aforesaid :

It shall be lawful for Her Majesty for that purpose to make provision, by way of regulations to be contained in any charter to be granted to the said Association, for the disposal of the lands to which the said terms of purchase and pasturage relate, so far as the same are still in force as aforesaid, and for varying from time to time such regulations, with such consent by or on behalf of the said Association as in any such charter

---

([1]) This transfer was effected in the year 1855. See the "Canterbury Associations Ordinance, Session IV., No. 6," (Canterbury).

or instructions shall be specified, and for fixing the boundaries thereof, and for enabling the said Association to transfer its powers to the Provincial Council for the Province of Otago : Provided always, that no such charter shall be granted or have effect for any longer term than ten years from the passing of this Act; but one of Her Majesty's Principal Secretaries of State may at any time during the term for which such charter shall be granted, by writing under his hand, extend the term for which such charter shall have been granted for such further time as in his discretion he may think fit : Provided always, that it shall not be lawful for Her Majesty, by any such regulations as aforesaid, to diminish the sum now payable to the New Zealand Company in respect of all waste land sold under the said terms of purchase, unless with the consent of the New Zealand Company, signified as hereinbefore provided ; and during the continuance of such charter as *No Act of the General Assembly to interfere with such regulations save with consent, &c.* aforesaid, it shall not be lawful for the said General Assembly to repeal or interfere with any such regulations respecting lands in Otago, except with such consent by or on behalf of the Otago Association as in any such charter or instructions may be provided, and (so far as the rights of the New Zealand Company may be affected) with the consent of such Company signified as hereinbefore provided ; and every Bill which shall repeal or interfere with any such regulations shall be reserved for the signification of Her Majesty's pleasure thereon.

79. It shall be lawful for Her Majesty, by any such *Her Majesty may delegate certain powers to Governor.* Letters Patent as aforesaid, or Instructions under Her Majesty's Signet and Sign Manual, or signified through one of Her Majesty's Principal Secretaries of State, to delegate to the Governor any of the powers hereinbefore reserved to Her Majesty respecting the removal of Superintendents of Provinces, and the regulation of the sale, letting, disposal, and occupation of waste lands, the establishment of municipal corporations, and the preservation of Aboriginal laws, customs, and usages.

80. (1) In the construction of this Act, the term *Interpretation of "Governor" and "New Zealand."* "Governor" shall mean the person for the time being lawfully administering the Government of New Zealand; and for the purposes of this Act "New Zealand" shall land."

(1) Amended by 26 and 27 Vict. c. 23 (Imperial), *post.*

be held to include all territories, islands, and countries lying between thirty-three degrees of South latitude and fifty degrees of South latitude, and one hundred and sixty-two degrees of East longitude and one hundred and seventy-three degrees of West longitude, reckoning from the meridian of Greenwich.

Commence-
ment of this
Act.

81. This Act shall be proclaimed in New Zealand by the Governor thereof within six weeks after a copy of such Act shall have been received by such Governor, [1] and, save as herein expressly provided, shall take effect in New Zealand from the day of such Proclamation thereof.

Proclamations
to be pub-
lished in *New
Zealand
Gazette.*

82. The Proclamation of this Act, and all Proclamations to be made under the provisions thereof, shall be published in the New Zealand Government *Gazette.*

SCHEDULE REFERRED TO IN THE FOREGOING ACT.

Governor	£2,500
Chief Justice	1,000
Puisné Judge	800
Establishment of the General Government...	4,700
Native Purposes	7,000
	£16,000

CONSTITUTION ACT AMENDMENT.
(20 & 21 VICT., CAP. LIII.)

AN ACT *to amend the Act for granting a Representative Constitution to the Colony of New Zealand.* [2]

[17th August, 1857.]

15 & 16 Vict.
c. 72.

WHEREAS it is expedient that an Act passed in the Session holden in the fifteenth and sixteenth years of Her Majesty, chapter seventy-two, to grant a Representative Constitution to the Colony of New Zealand, should be amended by repealing certain clauses thereof, whereby certain charges were imposed on the Territorial Revenue of the said Colony, for which charges other provision has been or is intended to be made, and

[1] It was proclaimed 17th January, 1853.
[2] The Short Title by which this Act is cited in New Zealand is " The Constitution Amendment Act." See the Interpretation Acts 1858 and 1868.

making further and other provision for enabling the General Assembly of New Zealand to alter the enactments thereof: BE IT ENACTED by the Queen's Most Excellent Majesty, by and with the advice and consent of the Lords Spiritual and Temporal, and Commons, in this present Parliament assembled, and by the authority of the same, as follows:

1. Sections sixty-seven, sixty-eight, sixty-nine, and seventy-four of the said Act of the fifteenth and sixteenth years of Her Majesty, and so much of section sixty-two of the said Act as authorizes and requires the Governor to pay out of the revenue arising from the disposal of waste lands of the Crown sums on account of the purchase of land from aboriginal natives, or the release or extinguishment of their rights, and sums payable to the New Zealand Company, are hereby repealed: *Sections 67, 68, 69, and 74, and part of sec. 62 of recited Act repealed.*

2. It shall be lawful for the said General Assembly of New Zealand, by any Act or Acts, from time to time to alter, suspend, or repeal all or any of the provisions of the said Act, except such as are hereinafter specified; [1] namely, *Power to General Assembly of New Zealand to vary the provisions of the recited Act, with the exception herein named.*

So much of the said Act as repeals former Acts, Letters Patent, Instructions, and Orders in Council:

The provisions contained in sections three, eighteen (save the exception therein contained), twenty-five, twenty-eight, twenty-nine, thirty-two, forty-four, forty-six, forty-seven, fifty-three, fifty-four, fifty-six, fifty-seven, fifty-eight, fifty-nine, sixty-one, sixty-four (save so much as charges the Civil List on the revenues arising from the disposal of waste lands of the Crown), sixty-five, seventy-one, seventy-three, and eighty of the said Act:

But no such Act of the General Assembly as aforesaid, which shall alter, suspend, or repeal any of the pro-

---

[1] As to the power of Colonial Legislatures generally to alter their constitution, see the Imperial Act 28 and 29 Vict. c. 63, s. 5, *post.* Power to alter the third section of the Constitution Act was given by the Imperial Act 24 and 25 Vict. c. 30, s. 2, *post ;* but that Act was repealed before the power was exercised. (See, *post*, the Imperial Act 25 and 26 Vict. c. 48.) Sect. 73 of the Constitution Act may be altered or repealed by the General Assembly (25 and 26 Vict. c. 48, s. 8).

5

visions contained in section nineteen of the said Act, shall have any force or effect unless the same shall have been reserved for the signification of Her Majesty's pleasure thereon, and until the Governor of New Zealand shall have signified, as provided by the said Act, that Her Majesty has been pleased to assent to the same.

Commence-
ment of Act.
3. This Act shall be proclaimed in New Zealand by the Governor, or person administering the Government thereof, within six weeks after a copy of such Act shall have been received by such Governor, and shall take effect in New Zealand from the day of such Proclamation;[1] except that the repeal of section seventy-four of the said recited Act, and of so much of section sixty-two as relates to sums payable to the New Zealand Company, shall only take effect if on or before the fifth day of April, one thousand eight hundred and fifty-eight, payment be made to the New Zealand Company of the sums and in the manner specified in the New Zealand Company's Claims Act, passed during the present Session of Parliament.[2]

(24 & 25 VICT., CAP. XXX.)

AN ACT *to declare the validity of an Act passed by the General Assembly of New Zealand, intituled "An Act to provide for the Establishment of new Provinces in New Zealand."*[3] [11th July, 1861.]

15 & 16 Vict.
c. 72.
WHEREAS by an Act of the Session holden in the fifteenth and sixteenth years of Her Majesty, intituled "An Act to grant a Representative Constitution to the Colony of New Zealand," it was provided that certain Provinces therein mentioned should be established in the said Colony, and that in every such Province there should be a Provincial Council, and that there should be in the said Colony a General Assembly competent to make laws for the peace, order, and good government of the same; and by the sixty-ninth section of the said Act it was further provided that it should be

----

[1] This Act was proclaimed on 15th December, 1857. See *Gazette* 1857, No. 34, page 195.
[2] This is " The New Zealand Company's Claims Act, 1857."
[3] This Act is repealed by 25 and 26 Vict. c. 48.

lawful for the said General Assembly to constitute new Provinces in the said Colony, and to appoint the number of Members of which the Provincial Councils thereof should consist, and to alter the boundaries of any Provinces for the time being existing, provided always that any Bill for any of the said purposes should be reserved for the signification of Her Majesty's pleasure thereon : And whereas by an Act of the Session holden in the twentieth and twenty-first years of Her Majesty, intituled "An Act to amend an Act for granting a Representative Constitution to the Colony of New Zealand," it was enacted that the sixty-ninth section of the said first-recited Act should be repealed, and that it should be lawful for the said General Assembly to alter, suspend, or repeal all or any of the provisions of the said Act, except the third section, and certain others therein specified : And whereas the said General Assembly, by an Act passed in a Session holden in the twenty-first and twenty-second years of Her Majesty, intituled "An Act to provide for the Establishment of new Provinces in New Zealand," did authorize the Governor of the said Colony to establish such new Provinces in manner therein mentioned, and the said Governor did establish certain new Provinces accordingly : And whereas doubts are entertained whether it was competent to the said General Assembly to make such provision, and to the said Governor to establish such new Provinces as aforesaid, and it is expedient that such doubts should be set at rest : And whereas it is also expedient that the said General Assembly should be at liberty to alter part of the third section of the hereinbefore first-recited Act of Parliament : BE IT THEREFORE ENACTED by the Queen's Most Excellent Majesty, by and with the advice and consent of the Lords Spiritual and Temporal, and Commons, in this present Parliament assembled, and by the authority of the same, as follows :—

20 & 21 Vict. c. 53.

1. It shall be lawful for the said General Assembly, by any Act or Acts to be by them from time to time passed, or for the Officer Administering the Government of New Zealand, acting under authority of any such Act or Acts, to constitute new Provinces in New

Power to General Assembly to constitute new Provinces.

Zealand, and to direct' and appoint the number of Members of which the Provincial Councils of such Provinces shall consist, and to alter the boundaries of any Provinces for the time being existing in New Zealand.

General Assembly may repeal part of sec. 3 of 15 & 16 Vict. c. 72. 2. It shall be lawful for the said General Assembly to alter, suspend, or repeal so much of the third section of the hereinbefore first-recited Act of Parliament as provides that the Provincial Council in each of the Provinces thereby established shall consist of such number of Members, not being less than nine, as the Governor shall by Proclamation appoint.

Recited Act of General Assembly, 21 & 22 Vict., to be valid. 3. The hereinbefore recited Act passed by the said General Assembly, and all acts, matters, or things done under and in pursuance of authority created or given, or expressed to be created or given, by the same Act, shall be, and shall be deemed to have been from the passing or doing thereof, as valid and effectual for all purposes whatever as such acts, matters, or things might or would have been if at the time of the passing of the same Act by the said General Assembly this Act of Parliament had been in force.

Recited Act to apply to new Provinces. 4. The provisions of the two hereinbefore recited Acts of Parliament, as altered by this Act, shall apply to all Provinces at any time existing in New Zealand, in like manner and under the same conditions as the same apply to the Provinces established by the hereinbefore first-recited Act of Parliament.

------◆------

(25 & 26 VICT., CAP. XLVIII.)

AN ACT *respecting the Establishment and Government of Provinces in New Zealand, and to enable the Legislature of New Zealand to repeal the Seventy-third Section of an Act intituled "An Act to grant a Representative Constitution to the Colony of New Zealand."*   [29th July, 1862.]

15 & 16 Vict. c. 72. WHEREAS by an Act of the Session holden in the fifteenth and sixteenth years of Her Majesty, intituled "An Act to grant a Representative Constitution to the Colony of New Zealand," it was provided that certain Provinces therein mentioned should be established in the said Colony, and that in every such Province there

should be a Provincial Council, and that there should
be in the said Colony a General Assembly competent
to make laws for the peace, order, and good government
of the same ; and by the sixty-ninth section of the said
Act it was further provided that it should be lawful for
the said General Assembly to constitute new Provinces
in the said Colony, and to appoint the number of Members of which the Provincial Councils thereof should
consist, and to alter the boundaries of any Provinces
for the time being existing : Provided always, that any
Bill for any of the said purposes should be reserved for
the signification of Her Majesty's pleasure thereon :
And whereas by an Act of the Session holden in the
twentieth and twenty-first years of Her Majesty, 20 & 21 Vict.
intituled " An Act to amend an Act for granting a c. 53.
Representative Constitution to the Colony of New
Zealand," it was enacted that the sixty-ninth section of
the said first-recited Act should be repealed, and that it
should be lawful for the said General Assembly to alter,
suspend, or repeal all or any of the provisions of the
said Act, except certain sections therein specified : And
whereas the said General Assembly, by an Act passed
in a Session holden in the twenty-first and twenty-
second years of Her Majesty, intituled "An Act to
provide for the Establishment of new Provinces in New
Zealand," or, more shortly, " The New Provinces Act,
1858," did authorize the Governor of the said Colony
to establish such new Provinces in manner therein
mentioned, and the said Governor did establish certain
new Provinces accordingly : And whereas doubts are
entertained whether it was competent to the said
General Assembly to make such provision, and to the
said Governor to establish such new Provinces as aforesaid : And whereas for the removing of such doubts
an Act was passed in the now last Session of Parliament,
intituled "An Act to declare the Validity of an Act 24 & 25 Vict.
passed by the General Assembly of New Zealand, c. 30.
intituled 'An Act to provide for the Establishment of
new Provinces in New Zealand':" And whereas it is
expedient to repeal the said last-mentioned Act of
Parliament, and to make fresh provision respecting the
establishment of new Provinces in New Zealand :
BE IT THEREFORE ENACTED by the Queen's Most

Excellent Majesty, by and with the advice and consent of the Lords Spiritual and Temporal, and Commons, in this present Parliament assembled, and by the authority of the same, as follows :

24 & 25 Vict. c. 30, repealed.
1. The said last-mentioned Act of Parliament shall be and the same is hereby repealed.

"New Provinces Act, 1858," confirmed.
2. The said "New Provinces Act, 1858," (except so far as the same shall have been altered by any Act subsequently passed by the said General Assembly,) shall be and be deemed to have been from the date of the passing thereof valid and effectual for all purposes whatever, and all matters and things done under and in pursuance of authority created or given, or expressed to be created or given by the same Act, shall be deemed to have been of the same force and effect as if the said Act, and everything therein contained, had from the above-mentioned date been actually so valid as aforesaid.

General Assembly to provide for the establishment of new Provinces in New Zealand.
3. Subject to the conditions hereinafter mentioned, it shall be lawful for the said General Assembly, by any Act or Acts to be by them from time to time passed, to establish or provide for the establishment of new Provinces in the Colony of New Zealand, and to alter or to provide for the alteration of the boundaries of any Provinces for the time being existing in the said Colony, and to make provision for the administration of any such Provinces, and for the passing of laws for the peace, order, and good government thereof, and therein to repeal or alter any of the provisions of the two first hereinbefore recited Acts of Parliament relating to such Provinces, or to the Superintendents and Provincial Councils thereof.

General Assembly not to make laws inconsistent with provisions herein mentioned.
4. It shall not be lawful for the General Assembly to make any law inconsistent with the following provisions; that is to say,

(1.) In every Province of New Zealand there shall be an officer designated the Superintendent, who, unless any provision shall be made to the contrary in any Act of the General Assembly, shall be capable of being elected and acting as a Member of the Council of the same Province.

(2.) No Provincial law shall take effect until it shall have received the assent in writing either of the said Superintendent or of the Governor of New Zealand.

(3.) In giving or refusing his assent to any Provincial law, or in reserving, the same for the signification of the Governor's pleasure, the Superintendent shall conform to such instructions in writing as he may from time to time receive from the Governor.

(4.) In case the Superintendent shall assent to any Provincial law, he shall forthwith transmit to the Governor an authentic copy thereof.

(5.) It shall be lawful for the Governor at any time after the date of such assent, and until the expiration of three months after such authentic copy of any Provincial law shall have been received by him, to declare by Proclamation his disallowance of such law, and such disallowance shall make void and annul the same from and after the day of the date of such Proclamation or any subsequent day to be named therein.

(6.) It shall not be lawful for the Council or other Legislative body of any Province to pass, or for the Superintendent or Governor to assent to, any Bill appropriating any money to the Public Service, unless the Superintendent or Governor shall first have recommended to the Council to make provision for the specific service to which such money is to be appropriated, and no such money shall be issued or made issuable except by warrants to be granted by the Superintendent or Governor.

(7.) It shall not be lawful for any such Council or other body as aforesaid to pass, and for the said Superintendent or Governor to assent to any law which shall be repugnant to the law of England or to any enactment of the said General Assembly.

5. It shall not be competent to the Governor of New Zealand to assent to any Bill passed by the Legislature of New Zealand which shall repeal or alter any of the provisions of the nineteenth clause of the first hereinbefore recited Act of Parliament, but the said Governor

Limitation of Governor's power to assent to Bills.

6

(unless he shall refuse his assent to such Bill) shall reserve the same for the signification of Her Majesty's pleasure.

Parts of two first-recited Acts repealed.
6. So much of the two first hereinbefore recited Acts of Parliament as is inconsistent with the provisions of this Act is hereby repealed.

Application of Acts to future Provinces.
7. Subject to the provisions of this Act and of the said New Provinces Act, the said two first hereinbefore recited Acts of Parliament shall apply to all Provinces at any time existing in New Zealand, in like manner and subject to the same conditions as the same apply to Provinces established by the first hereinbefore recited Act of Parliament.

Power to General Assembly to repeal or alter sec. 73 of 15 and 16 Vict. c. 72.
8. And whereas it is expedient to enable the General Assembly of New Zealand to repeal the seventy-third section of the first hereinbefore recited Act of Parliament : Be it further enacted as follows (that is to say) : It shall be lawful for the said General Assembly to alter or repeal all or any of the provisions contained in the said section; and no Act passed by the General Assembly, nor any part of such Act, shall be or be deemed to have been invalid by reason that the same is repugnant to any of the said provisions.

" Governor."
9. In the construction of this Act the term " Governor " shall mean the person for the time being lawfully administering the Government of New Zealand.

------◆------

(26 & 27 VICT., CAP. XXIII.)

An Act to alter the Boundaries of New Zealand.
[8th June, 1863.]

15 & 16 Vict. c. 72.
WHEREAS by the eightieth section of an Act of the fifteenth year of Her Majesty, chapter seventy-two, intituled, " An Act to grant a Representative Constitution to the Colony of New Zealand," it was provided, that for the purposes of that Act the said Colony should be held to include the Territories therein mentioned : And whereas it is expedient to alter the limits of the said Colony as declared by the said Act :

BE IT THEREFORE ENACTED by the Queen's Most Excellent Majesty, by and with the advice and consent of the Lords Spiritual and Temporal, and Commons, in this present Parliament assembled, and by the authority of the same, as follows :

1. So much of the eightieth section of the aforesaid Part of Act of Parliament as declares the limits of the Colony sec. 80 of of New Zealand for the purposes of the said Act is 15 & 16 Vict. c. 72 repealed. repealed.

2. The Colony of New Zealand shall for the purposes What shall be of the said Act and for all other purposes whatever deemed the be deemed to comprise all Territories, Islands, and Colony. Countries lying between the one hundred and sixty-second degree of East longitude and the one hundred and seventy-third degree of West longitude, and between the thirty-third and fifty-third parallels of South latitude.

(28 & 29 VICT., CAP. LXIII.)

AN ACT *to remove Doubts as to the Validity of Colonial Laws.* [29th June, 1865.]

WHEREAS doubts have been entertained respecting the validity of divers laws enacted or purporting to have been enacted by the Legislatures of certain of Her Majesty's Colonies, and respecting the powers of such Legislatures, and it is expedient that such doubts should be removed :

BE IT HEREBY ENACTED by the Queen's Most Excellent Majesty, by and with the advice and consent of the Lords Spiritual and Temporal, and Commons, in this present Parliament assembled, and by the authority of the same, as follows :

1. The term " Colony " shall in this Act include all Definitions— of Her Majesty's possessions abroad in which there " Colony." shall exist a Legislature, as hereinafter defined, except the Channel Islands, the Isle of Man, and such territories as may for the time being be vested in Her Majesty under or by virtue of any Act of Parliament for the Government of India :

The terms " Legislature" and "Colonial Legislature" " Legisla. shall severally signify the authority, other than the ture." " Colonial Imperial Parliament or Her Majesty in Council, com- Legislature." petent to make laws for any Colony :

The term " Representative Legislature " shall signify " Representa- any Colonial Legislature which shall comprise a Legis- tive Legisla- lative Body of which one-half are elected by inhabitants ture." of the Colony :

The term " Colonial Law " shall include laws made " Colonial for any Colony either by such Legislature as aforesaid Law." or by Her Majesty in Council :

Act of Parliament, &c., when to extend to Colony. An Act of Parliament, or any provision thereof, shall, in construing this Act, be said to extend to any Colony when it is made applicable to such Colony by the express words or necessary intendment of any Act of Parliament:

"Governor." The term " Governor " shall mean the officer lawfully administering the Government of any Colony :

"Letters Patent." The terms " Letters Patent " shall mean Letters Patent under the Great Seal of the United Kingdom of Great Britain and Ireland.

Colonial Law, when void for repugnancy. 2. Any Colonial Law which is or shall be in any respect repugnant to the provisions of any Act of Parliament extending to the Colony to which such law may relate, or repugnant to any Order or Regulation made under authority of such Act of Parliament, or having in the Colony the force and effect of such Act, shall be read subject to such Act, Order, or Regulation, and shall, to the extent of such repugnancy, but not otherwise, be and remain absolutely void and inoperative.

Colonial Law, when not void for repugnancy. 3. No Colonial Law shall be or be deemed to have been void or inoperative on the ground of repugnancy to the Law of England, unless the same shall be repugnant to the provisions of some such Act of Parliament, Order, or Regulation as aforesaid.

Colonial Law not void for inconsistency with instructions. 4. No Colonial Law, passed with the concurrence of or assented to by the Governor of any Colony, or to be hereafter so passed or assented to, shall be or be deemed to have been void or inoperative by reason only of any instructions with reference to such law or the subject thereof which may have been given to such Governor by or on behalf of Her Majesty, by any instrument other than the Letters Patent or instrument authorizing such Governor to concur in passing or to assent to laws for the peace, order, and good government of such Colony, even though such instructions may be referred to in such Letters Patent or last-mentioned instrument.

Colonial Legislature may establish, &c., Courts of Law. 5. Every Colonial Legislature shall have and be deemed at all times to have had, full power within its jurisdiction to establish Courts of Judicature, and to abolish and reconstitute the same, and to alter the constitution thereof, and to make provision for the administration of Justice therein, and every Representative Legislature, shall, in respect to the Colony under its jurisdiction, have, and be deemed at all times to have had, full power to make laws respecting the constitution, powers, and procedure of such Legislature; provided that such laws shall have been passed in such manner and form as may from time to time be required by any Act of Parliament, Letters Patent, Order in Council, or Colonial Law for the time being in force in the said Colony.

6. The certificate of the Clerk or other proper officer *Representa-* of a Legislative Body in any Colony, to the effect that *tive Legisla-* the document to which it is attached is a true copy of *ture may alter* any Colonial Law assented to by the Governor of such *constitution.* Colony, or of any Bill reserved for the signification of Her Majesty's pleasure by the said Governor, shall be *primâ facie* evidence that the document so certified is a true copy of such Law or Bill, and, as the case may be, that such law has been duly and properly passed and assented to, or that such Bill has been duly and properly passed and presented to the Governor; and any Proclamation purporting to be published by authority of the Governor in any newspaper in the Colony to which such Law or Bill shall relate, and signifying Her Majesty's disallowance of any such Colonial Law, or Her Majesty's assent to any such reserved Bill as aforesaid, shall be *primâ facie* evidence of such disallowance or assent.

7. [*Certain Acts of Legislature of South Australia to be valid.*]

———————◆———————

(31 & 32 VICT., CAP. LVII.)

AN ACT *to make Provision for the Appointment of Members of the Legislative Council of New Zealand, and to remove Doubts in respect of past Appointments.* [13th July, 1868.]

WHEREAS by an Act passed in the Session of Par- 15 & 16 Vict. liament holden in the fifteenth and sixteenth years of c. 72. Her Majesty's reign, chapter seventy-two, intituled " An Act to grant a Representative Constitution to the Colony of New Zealand," it is (amongst other things) enacted, that it shall be lawful for Her Majesty, from time to time, by any instrument under her Royal Sign Manual, to authorize the Governor to summon to the Legislative Council of the said Colony such person or persons as Her Majesty shall think fit, being qualified as therein is mentioned :

And whereas Her Majesty has, by divers instruments under her Royal Sign Manual, authorized successive Governors of the said Colony to summon to the said Legislative Council, from time to time, such person or persons, being qualified as aforesaid, as the said Governors respectively should deem to be prudent and discreet men :

And whereas, in pursuance of the said instructions, persons have, from time to time, been summoned to the said Legislative Council by the Governors of the said Colony :

And whereas doubts have arisen whether such persons, not having been, previously to their being so summoned, expressly named or appointed by Her Majesty in any instrument under the Royal Sign Manual, or otherwise, have been legally summoned to the said Legislative Council, and become Members thereof ; and it is expedient that such doubts should be removed, and that fresh provision should be made for the future appointment of Legislative Councillors in the said Colony :

Be it enacted by the Queen's Most Excellent Majesty, by and with the advice and consent of the Lords Spiritual and Temporal, and Commons, in this present Parliament assembled, and by the authority of the same, as follows :

Part of recited Act repealed. 1. So much of the said recited Act as is inconsistent with this Act is hereby repealed :

Governor empowered to summon such persons as he may think fit to the Legislative Council. 2. From and after the proclamation of this Act in the said Colony of New Zealand,([1]) it shall be lawful for the Governor of the said Colony, from time to time, in Her Majesty's name, by an instrument or instruments under the Public Seal of the said Colony, to summon to the said Legislative Council such person or persons as the said Governor shall think fit, either in addition to the present Members of the said Council, or for supplying any vacancies which may take place therein by death or otherwise ; and every person who shall be so summoned shall thereby become a Member of the Legislative Council : Provided always, that, unless otherwise de-

---

([1]) This Act was proclaimed on 29th January, 1869. See *New Zealand Gazette*, 1869, p. 35.

termined by the Legislature of New Zealand, no person shall be summoned to such Legislative Council who shall not be of the full age of twenty-one years, and either a natural-born subject of Her Majesty, or a subject of Her Majesty naturalized by Act of Parliament or by an Act of the Legislature of New Zealand.

3. All persons who, before the proclamation of this Act in the said Colony, shall have been summoned to the Legislative Council of the said Colony by the Governor without having been so previously named or appointed by Her Majesty as aforesaid shall be deemed and taken to have been legally summoned, and to be and to have been and become Members of the Legislative Council from the respective periods when they were so summoned; and no matter or thing done by any such person so summoned as aforesaid, as such Member as aforesaid, shall be deemed or taken to be or to have been invalid by reason of such person not having been previously duly named or appointed by Her Majesty in pursuance of the said recited Act. *All summonses to Legislative Council declared valid.*

4. In the construction of this Act the term "Governor" shall mean the person for the time being lawfully administering the Government of New Zealand. *"Governor."*

----◆----

(31 & 32 VICT., CAP. XCII.)

AN ACT *to declare the Powers of the General Assembly of New Zealand to abolish any Province in that Colony, or to withdraw from any such Province any part of the Territory thereof.*(¹) [31st July, 1868.[

WHEREAS by the third section of an Act of the Session holden in the twenty-fifth and twenty-sixth years of Her Majesty, intituled "An Act respecting the Establishment and Government of Provinces in New Zealand, and to enable the Legislature of New Zealand to repeal the seventy-third section of an Act intituled 'An Act to grant a Representative Constitution to the Colony of New Zealand,'" it was provided that it shall be lawful for the General Assembly of New Zealand, by any Act or Acts to be by them from time to time passed, to *25 & 26 Vict. c. 48, s. 3.*

(¹) This Act was rendered necessary by doubts as to the validity of " The County of Westland Act, 1867."

establish or provide for the establishment of new Provinces in the Colony of New Zealand, and to alter or
to provide for the alteration of the boundaries of any
Provinces for the time being existing in the said Colony,
and to make provision for the administration of any
such Provinces, and for the passing of laws for the
peace, order, and good government thereof: And
whereas doubts are entertained whether the said General
Assembly has power under the above-recited enactments, or otherwise, to abolish any such Province now
or hereafter to be established, or to withdraw from such
Province any part of the territory comprised therein,
except for the purpose of including the same within the
limits of some other such Province, and it is expedient
that such doubts should be removed :

BE IT THEREFORE ENACTED by the Queen's Most Excellent Majesty, by and with the advice and consent
of the Lords Spiritual and Temporal, and Commons,
in this present Parliament assembled, and by the
authority of the same, as follows :

General As-
sembly to have
and to be
deemed to
have had
power to
abolish any
Province, to
withdraw
therefrom any
territory, and
to make laws
for such terri-
tory.

1. The General Assembly of New Zealand shall be
deemed to have, and since the passing of the afore-
mentioned Act to have had, the power of abolishing
any Province at any time heretofore or hereafter to be
established in New Zealand, or of withdrawing therefrom
the whole or any part of the territory comprised therein,
and of passing laws for the peace, order, and good
government of the territory so withdrawn from or
ceasing to form part of the territory of any such Province, whether such territory shall or shall not be
included within the limits of any other Province of New
Zealand, and also the power of making from time to
time such provision as to such General Assembly shall
seem expedient, relating to the effect and operation of
any such withdrawals of territory in or with respect to
the Province from which such territory shall have been
withdrawn, and the Superintendent and Members of the
Provincial Council thereof for the time being in office,
and the laws in force in such Province at the time of
such withdrawals of territory therefrom.